ALSO BY CHARLES WRIGHT

Poetry

The Grave of the Right Hand
Hard Freight
Bloodlines
China Trace
The Southern Cross
Country Music: Selected Early Poems
The Other Side of the River
Zone Journals
Xionia
The World of the Ten Thousand Things: Poems 1980–1990
Chickamauga
Black Zodiac
Appalachia
North American Bear
Negative Blue: Selected Later Poems
A Short History of the Shadow
Buffalo Yoga
Littlefoot

Translations

The Storm and Other Things (Eugenio Montale)
Orphic Songs (Dino Campana)

Nonfiction

Halflife
Quarter Notes

SCAR TISSUE

SCAR TISSUE

Charles Wright

Farrar, Straus and Giroux   New York

Farrar, Straus and Giroux
18 West 18th Street, New York 10011

Copyright © 2006 by Charles Wright

Printed in the United States of America
Published in 2006 by Farrar, Straus and Giroux
First paperback edition, 2007

Grateful acknowledgment is made to the following publications, in whose pages these poems
first appeared: *Appalachian Heritage, Blackbird, Daedalus, Davidson College Broadside
Series, Field, The Iowa Review, Irish Pages, The Kenyon Review, The Literary Review, Meridian, The New Yorker, The Notre Dame Review, The Paris Review, Pima Press, Poetry, Poets on
Place* (Utah University Press), *Shenandoah, Verse, The Virginia Quarterly Review, Visions-International* (Black Buzzard Press), and *West Branch*.

Part 1 and two poems from Part 3 were printed by Sarabande Press as a chapbook, *The
Wrong End of the Rainbow*, in 2005.

The Library of Congress has cataloged the hardcover edition as follows:
Wright, Charles, 1935–
    Scar tissue / Charles Wright.— 1st ed.
    p. cm.
    Includes bibliographical references.
    ISBN-13: 978-0-374-25427-8 (alk. paper)
    ISBN-10: 0-374-25427-3 (alk. paper)
    I. Title

PS3573.R52S33 2006
811'.54—dc22
                                        2005052259

Paperback ISBN-13: 978-0-374-53083-9
Paperback ISBN-10: 0-374-53083-1

Designed by Jonathan D. Lippincott

www.fsgbooks.com

For Chuck and Ditty, for John and Jeanette, in gratitude.
Mountains and rivers and lakes and things . . .

Contents

1

Appalachian Farewell

Sunset in Appalachia, bituminous bulwark
Against the western skydrop.
An Advent of gold and green, an Easter of ashes.

If night is our last address,
This is the place we moved from,
Backs on fire, our futures hard-edged and sure to arrive.

These are the towns our lives abandoned,
Wind in our faces,
The idea of incident like a box beside us on the Trailways seat.

And where were we headed for?
The country of Narrative, that dark territory
Which spells out our stories in sentences, which gives them an end
                                        and beginning . . .

Goddess of Bad Roads and Inclement Weather, take down
Our names, remember us in the drip
And thaw of the wintry mix, remember us when the light cools.

Help us never to get above our raising, help us
To hold hard to what was there,
Orebank and Reedy Creek, Surgoinsville down the line.

Last Supper

I seem to have come to the end of something, but don't know what,
Full moon blood orange just over the top of the redbud tree.
Maundy Thursday tomorrow,
                              Then Good Friday, then Easter in full drag,
Dogwood blossoms like little crosses
All down the street,
                    lilies and jonquils bowing their mitred heads.

Perhaps it's a sentimentality about such fey things,
But I don't think so. One knows
There is no end to the other world,
                                no matter where it is.
In the event, a reliquary evening for sure,
The bones in their tiny boxes, rosettes under glass.

Or maybe it's just the way the snow fell
                              a couple of days ago,
So white on the white snowdrops.
As our fathers were bold to tell us,
                              it's either eat or be eaten.
Spring in its starched bib,
Winter's cutlery in its hands. Cold grace. Slice and fork.

Inland Sea

Little windows of gold paste,
Long arm of the Archer high above.
Cross after cross on the lawn. Dry dreams. Leftover light.
Bitter the waters of memory,
Bitter their teeth and cold lips.

Better to stuff your heart with dead moss,
Better to empty your mouth of air
Remembering Babylon
Than to watch those waters rise
And fall, and to hear their suck and sigh.

Nostalgia arrives like a spring storm,
Looming and large with fine flash,
Dissolving like a disease then
                        into the furred horizon,
Whose waters have many doors,
Whose sky has a thousand panes of glass.

Nighttime still dogs and woos us
With tiny hiccups and tiny steps,
The constellations ignore our moans,
The tulip flames
                    snuffed in their dark cups,
No cries of holy, holy, holy.

Little windows of gold paste,
Long arm of the Archer high above.
Cross after cross on the lawn. Dry dreams. Leftover light.

Bitter the waters of memory,
Bitter their teeth and cold lips.

The Silent Generation II

We've told our story. We told it twice and took our lumps.
You'll find us here, of course, at the end of the last page,
Our signatures scratched in smoke.

Thunderstorms light us and roll on by.
Branches bend in the May wind,
But don't snap, the flowers bend and do snap, the grass gorps.

And then the unaltered grey,
Uncymbaled, undrumrolled, no notes to set the feet to music.
Still, we pull it up to our chins; it becomes our lives.

Garrulous, word-haunted, senescent,
Who knew we had so much to say, or tongue to say it?
The wind, I guess, who's heard it before, and crumples our pages.

And so we keep on, stiff lip, slack lip,
Hoping for words that are not impermanent—small words,
Out of the wind and the weather—that will not belie our names.

High Country Canticle

The shroud has no pockets, the northern Italians say.
Let go, live your life,
                    the grave has no sunny corners—
Deadfall and windfall, the aphoristic undertow
Of high water, deep snow in the hills,
Everything's benediction, bright wingrush of grace.

Spring moves through the late May heat
                              as though someone were poling it.

The Wrong End of the Rainbow

It must have been Ischia, Forio d'Ischia.
Or Rome. The Pensione Margutta. Or Naples
Somewhere, on some dark side street in 1959

With What's-Her-Name, dear golden-haired What's-Her-Name.
                                          Or Yes-Of-Course
In Florence, in back of S. Maria Novella,
And later wherever the Carabinieri let us lurk.

Milano, with That's-The-One, two streets from the Bar Giamaica.
Venice and Come-On-Back,
                        three flights up,
Canal as black as an onyx, and twice as ground down.

Look, we were young then, and the world would sway to our sway.
We were riverrun, we were hawk's breath.
Heart's lid, we were center's heat at the center of things.

Remember us as we were, amigo,
And not as we are, stretched out at the wrong end of the rainbow,
Our feet in the clouds,
                        our heads in the small, still pulse-pause of age,

Gazing out of some window, still taking it all in,
Our arms around Memory,
Her full lips telling us just those things
                                she thinks we want to hear.

A Field Guide to the Birds of the Upper Yaak

A misty rain, no wind from the west,
Clouds close as smoke to the ground,
                         spring's fire, like a first love, now gone to ash,
The lives of angels beginning to end like porch lights turned off
From time zone to time zone,
                         our pictures still crooked on the walls,
Our prayer, like a Chinese emperor, always two lips away,
Our pockets gone dry and soft with lint.
Montana morning, a cold front ready to lay its ears back.

If I were a T'ang poet, someone would bid farewell
At this point, or pluck a lute string,
                         or knock on a hermit's door.
I'm not, and there's no one here.
The iconostasis of evergreens across the two creeks
Stands dark, unkissed and ungazed upon.
Tonight, it's true, the River of Heaven will cast its net of strung stars,
But that's just the usual stuff.
                  As I say, there's no one here.

In fact, there's almost never another soul around.
There are no secret lives up here,
                       it turns out, everything goes
Its own way, its only way,
Out in the open, unexamined, unput upon.
The great blue heron unfolds like a pterodactyl
Over the upper pond,
                two robins roust a magpie,
Snipe snipe, the swallows wheel, and nobody gives a damn.

A Short History of My Life

Unlike Lao-tzu, conceived of a shooting star, it is said,
And carried inside his mother's womb
For 62 years, and born, it's said once again, with white hair,
I was born on a Sunday morning,
                    untouched by the heavens,
Some hair, no teeth, the shadows of twilight in my heart,
And a long way from the way.
Shiloh, the Civil War battleground, was just next door,
The Tennessee River soft shift at my head and feet.
The dun-colored buffalo, the sands of the desert,
Gatekeeper and characters,
                    were dragon years from then.

Like Dionysus, I was born for a second time.
From the flesh of Italy's left thigh, I emerged one January
Into a different world.
                It made a lot of sense,
Hidden away, as I had been, for almost a life.
And I entered it open-eyed, the wind in my ears,
The slake of honey and slow wine awake on my tongue.
Three years I stood in S. Zeno's doors,
                and took, more Rome than Rome,
Whatever was offered me.
The snows of the Dolomites advanced to my footfalls.
The lemons of Lago di Garda fell to my hands.

Fast-forward some forty-five years,
                and a third postpartum blue.
But where, as the poet asked, will you find it in history?

Alluding to something else.
Nowhere but here, my one and only, nowhere but here.
My ears and my sick senses seem pure with the sound of water.
I'm back, and it's lilac time,
The creeks running eastward unseen through the dank morning,
Beginning of June. No light on leaf,
No wind in the evergreens, no bow in the still-blonde grasses.
The world in its dark grace.
        I have tried to record it.

Waking Up After the Storm

It's midnight. The cloud-glacier breaks up,
Thunder-step echoes off to the east,
                              and flashes like hoof sparks.
Someone on horseback leaving my dream.

Senseless to wonder who it might be, and what he took.
Senseless to rummage around in the light-blind stars.
                                                    Already
The full moon is one eye too many.

Images from the Kingdom of Things

Sunlight is blowing westward across the unshadowed meadow,
Night, in its shallow puddles,
                                            still liquid and loose in the trees.
The world is a desolate garden,
No distillation of downed grasses,
                        no stopping the clouds, coming at us one by one.

———————

The snow crown on Mt. Henry is still white,
                                            the old smoke watcher's tower
Left-leaning a bit in its odd angle to the world,
Abandoned, unusable.
Down here, in their green time, it's past noon
                        and the lodgepole pines adjust their detonators.

———————

The blanched bones of moonlight scatter across the meadow.
The song of the second creek, with its one note,
                                            plays over and over.
How many word-warriors ever return
                                    from midnight's waste and ruin?
Count out the bones, count out the grains in the yellow dust.

Confessions of a Song and Dance Man

The wind is my music, the west wind, and cold water
In constant motion.
                        I have an ear
For such things, and the sound of the goatsucker at night.
And the click of twenty-two cents in my pants pocket
That sets my feet to twitching,
                        that clears space in my heart.

"We are nothing but footmen at the coach of language,
We open and close the door."
                        Hmmm two three, hmmm two three.
"Only the language is evergreen,
                        everything else is seasonal."
A little time step, a little back-down on the sacred harp.
"Language has many mothers, but only one father."

————————

The dying *narcissus poeticus* by the cabin door,
Bear grass, like Dante's souls,
                        flame-flicked throughout the understory,
The background humdrum of mist
Like a Chinese chant and character among the trees,
Like dancers wherever the wind comes on and lifts them . . .

The stillness of what's missing
                        after the interwork's gone,
A passing sand step, a slow glide and hush to the wings—
A little landscape's a dangerous thing, it seems,

Giving illusion then taking it back,
                    a sleight of hand tune
On a pennywhistle, but holding the measure still, holding the time.

A God-fearing agnostic,
                    I tend to look in the corners of things,
Those out-of-the-way places,
The half-dark and half-hidden,
                    the passed-by and over-looked,
Whenever I want to be sure I can't find something.
I go out of my way to face them and pin them down.

Are you there, Lord, I whisper,
                    knowing he's not around,
Mumble *kyrie eleison*, mumble O three-in-none.
Distant thunder of organ keys
In the fitful, unoccupied
                    cathedral of memory.
Under my acolyte's robes, a slip-step and glide, slip-step and a glide.

Red-winged blackbird balancing back and forth on pond reed,
Back and forth then off then back again.
What is it he's after,
                    wing-hinge yellow and orange,
What is it he needs down there
In snipe country, marsh-muddled,
                    rinsed in long-day sunlight?

The same thing I need up here, I guess,
A place to ruffle and strut,
                    a place to perch and sing.

I sit by the west window, the morning building its ruins
In increments, systematically, across the day's day.

Make my bed and light the light,
I'll be home late tonight, blackbird, bye-bye.

Against the American Grain

Stronger and stronger, the sunlight glues
The afternoon to its objects,
                      the baby pine tree,
The scapular shadow thrown over the pond and meadow grass,
The absence the two
                horses have left on the bare slope,
The silence that grazes like two shapes where they have been.

The slow vocabulary of sleep
                          spits out its consonants
And drifts in its vowely weather,
Sun-pocked, the afternoon dying among its odors,
The cocaine smell of the wind,
The too-sweet and soft-armed
                        fragrance around the reluctant lilac bush.

Flecked in the underlap, however,
                        half-glimpsed, half-recognized,
Something unordinary persists,
Something unstill, never-sleeping, just possible past reason.
Then unflecked by evening's overflow
                        and its counter current.
What mystery can match its maliciousness, what moan?

College Days

Mooresville, North Carolina, September 1953.
Hearts made of stone, doodly wop, doodly wop, will never break . . . I
Should have paid more attention, *doodly wop, doodly wop,*
To the words and not just the music.
Stonestreet's Cafe,
                    the beginning of what might be loosely called
My life of learning and post-adolescent heartbreak-without-borders.
All I remember now is four years of Pabst Blue Ribbon beer,
A novel or two, and the myth of Dylan Thomas—
American lay by, the academic chapel and parking lot.
O, yes, and my laundry number, 597.

What does it say about me that what I recall best
Is a laundry number—
                    that only reality endures?
Hardly. Still, it's lovely to hope so,
That speculation looms like an ever-approaching event
Darkly on the horizon,
                    and bids us take shelter,
Though, like Cavafy's barbarians, does not arrive.
That's wishful thinking, Miguel,
But proper, I guess,
                    to small rooms and early morning hours,
Where juke joints and clean clothes come in as a second best.
Is sin, as I said one time, more tactile than a tree?

Some things move in and dig down
                                whether you want them to or not.
Like pieces of small glass your body subsumes when you are young,

They exit transformed and easy-edged
Many years later, in middle age, when you least expect them,
And shine like Lot's redemption.
College is like this, a vast, exact,
                              window of stained glass
That shatters without sound as you pass,
Year after year disappearing, unnoticed and breaking off.
Gone, you think, when you are gone, thank God. But look again.
Already the glass is under your skin,
                              already the journey's on.

There is some sadness involved, but not much.
                              Nostalgia, too, but not much.
Those years are the landscape of their own occasions, nothing lost,
It turns out, the solemn sentences metabolized
Into the truths and tacky place mats
We lay out
            when custom demands it.
That world becomes its own image, for better or worse
—the raven caws, the Weed-Eater drones—
And has no objective correlative to muscle it down.
It floats in the aether of its own content,
                              whose grass we lie on,
Listening to nothing. And to its pale half brother, the nothingness.

Night Thoughts Under a China Moon

Out here, where the clouds pass without end,
One could walk in any direction till water cut the trail,
The Hunter Gracchus in his long body
                              approaching along the waves
Each time in his journey west of west.

Bedtime Story

The generator hums like a distant *ding an sich*.
It's early evening, and time, like the dog it is,
                                              is hungry for food,
And will be fed, don't doubt it, will be fed, my small one.
The forest begins to gather its silences in.
The meadow regroups and hunkers down
                                   for its cleft feet.

Something is wringing the rag of sunlight
                                    inexorably out and hanging.
Something is making the reeds bend and cover their heads.
Something is licking the shadows up,
And stringing the blank spaces along, filling them in.
Something is inching its way into our hearts,
                        scratching its blue nails against the wall there.

Should we let it in?
                 Should we greet it as it deserves,
Hands on our ears, mouths open?
Or should we bring it a chair to sit on, and offer it meat?
Should we turn on the radio,
                        should we clap our hands and dance
The Something Dance, the welcoming Something Dance?
                        I think we should, love, I think we should.

Transparencies

Our lives, it seems, are a memory
                                we had once in another place.
Or are they its metaphor?
The trees, if trees they are, seem the same,
                                and the creeks do.
The sunlight blurts its lucidity in the same way,
And the clouds, if clouds they really are,
                                still follow us,
One after one, as they did in the old sky, in the old place.

I wanted the metaphor, if metaphor it is, to remain
                                always the same one.
I wanted the hills to be the same,
And the rivers too,
                especially the old rivers,
The French Broad and Little Pigeon, the Holston and Tennessee,
And me beside them, under the stopped clouds and stopped stars.
I wanted to walk in that metaphor,
                                untouched by time's corruption.

I wanted the memory adamantine, never-changing.
I wanted the memory amber,
                                and me in it,
A figure among its translucent highlights and swirls,
Mid-stride in its glittery motions.
I wanted the memory cloud-sharp and river-sharp,
My place inside it transfiguring, ever-still,
                                no wind and no wave.

But memory has no memory. Or metaphor.
It moves as it wants to move,
                                    and never measures the distance.
People have died of thirst in crossing a memory.
Our lives are summer cotton, it seems,
                                    and good for a season.
The wind blows, the rivers run, and waves come to a head.
Memory's logo is the abyss, and that's no metaphor.

Morning Occurrence at Xanadu

Swallows are flying grief-circles over their featherless young,
Night-dropped and dead on the wooden steps.
The aspen leaves have turned grey,
                                        slapped by the hard, west wind.

Someone who knows how little he knows
Is like the man who comes to a clearing in the forest,
                                        and sees the light spikes,
And suddenly senses how happy his life has been.

Saturday Morning Satori

When the mind is exalted, the body is lightened, the Chinese say,
Or one of them said,
                          and feels as though it could float in the wind.
Neglecting to say like what, I think it might be like a leaf,
Like this leaf in careless counterpoint
                                                down from an unseen tree,
West wind deep bass line under raven shrill.
                                         No, it's a feather,

One thing in a world of images.
It's not a question of what we think, we think too much.
It's not a question of what we say, we say too much.
A thing is not an image,
                          imagination's second best,
A language in which the heavens call out to us
                                         each day in their gutterals.

Wrong Notes

To bring the night sky to life,
                                    strike a wrong note from time to time,
Half for the listening ear, half for the watching eye.
Up here, just north of the Cabinet Mountains,
                                    the Great Bear
Seems closer to me than the equinox, or rinsed glints
In the creek hurrying elsewhere into evening's undergrowth.

The same way with the landscape.
                                    Our meadow, for instance,
Has two creeks that cross it;
                                    they join and become one about halfway down.
And that runs under my west window.
These are the flash and lapped scales
That trouble the late sunlight,
                                    and spark the moon fires and moon dregs.

At other times, it seems invisible, or they do,
Moving slowly in dark slides
                                    from beaver break to beaver break,
Muscling down from spruce shadow through willow shadow.
Above its margins the deer graze,
                                    two coyotes skulk and jump,
And clouds start to herd together like wounded cattle.

And what does this matter?
                                    Not much, unless you're one of those,
As I am, who hears a music in such things, who thinks,
When the sun goes down, or the stars do,

That the tune they're doing is his song,
That the instruments of the given world
                                    play only for him.

The Minor Art of Self-defense

Landscape was never a subject matter, it was a technique,
A method of measure,
                        a scaffold for structuring.
I stole its silences, I stepped to its hue and cry.

Language was always the subject matter, the idea of God
The ghost that over my little world
Hovered, my mouthpiece for meaning,
                              my claw and bright beak . . .

2

Scar Tissue

What must be said can't be said,
It looks like; nobody has a clue,
                    not even, it seems, the landscape.
One hears it in dreams, they say,
Or out of the mouths of oracles, or out of the whirlwind.

I thought I heard it, a whisper, once,
In the foothills of the Dolomites,
                    night and a starless sky,
But who can remember, a black night, a starless sky,
Blurred voice and a blurred conceit.

It takes a crack in the membrane,
                    a tiny crack, a stain,
To let it come through; a breath, a breath like a stopped sigh
From the land of foreign tongues.
It is what it has to say, sad stain of our fathers.

Whatever is insignificant has its own strength,
Whatever is hidden, clear vision.
Thus the ant in its hide-and-seek,
                    thus the dung beetle,
And all the past weight of the world it packs on its back.

The insect world has no tongue to let loose, and no tongue to curb,
Though all day and all night it cries out.
Who says we shouldn't listen to them?
Who says we shouldn't behave ourselves as they do,
                    no noise but for one purpose?

Whatever the root sees in the dark is infinite.
Whatever the dead see is the same.
Listen, the rivers are emptying
                    under our feet,
Watched over by all the waters of the underworld.

————————

Why does one never tire of looking out at the obvious?
The merely picturesque
                    is good for a day or so,
The ugly fascinates for a little while, then scabs over, like grease.
Only the obvious, with its odd neck, holds us close,

The endless sky with its endless cargo of cloud parts,
The wind in the woebegone of summer afternoons,
The landscape in its last lurch,
The shadowy overkill
                    of the evening sun going down.

It seems, somehow, to ignite us into a false love for the physical world.
Our mouths full of ashes, our mouths full of fresh fire,
                                        phoenix-like,
Wide wings over wider lives,
We open and close on demand, we open and close.

————————

The woods are thick with sunlight.
Tonight, over the mountain,
                    the full moon will replenish them
With their own reflected face.

————————

This is the almost hour,
                    almost darkness, almost light,
Far northern dusk dust sifting over the evergreens,

Chiaroscuro at heaven's walk,
Charcoal and deeper shades where our foot falls and hands hang.

This is the time of mixed masks.
This is the time of sour songs,
                              of love gone wrong, of sixes and sevens,
The almost hour, the zero-zero.
This is the one place we feel at home, this is our zone.

The idea of horses grazes in deep, black grass.
The idea of separation
                        unleashes its luminous line
That holds us at either end.
How happy we are here, how utterly dark our contentment.

—————

Friday, a little perch, a branch, to rest on for a moment.
Yesterday, Thursday,
I rose and fell like a firefly,
                        light off, light back on.
Today, I'm a hummingbird
On Friday's slick branch,
                  my heart like a beat machine, my wings a green itch.

—————

It is impossible to say good-bye to the past.
Whose images are they anyway,
                        whose inability to spell them out?
Such destitution of words.
What hand was seen to wave in the all-absorbing light?

Better to leave it alone.
Better to let it drift there,
                  at the end edge of sight,

Replete with its angel bands and its handsful of golden hair,
Just out of earshot, just out of reach.

But someday that hand will reappear
Out of the awful blear-light.
Someday that hand, white hand in the white light,
                                   will wave again, and not stop.
No reason to look around then, it will be waving to you.

_____

The slit wrists of sundown
                        tincture the western sky wall,
The drained body of daylight trumps the Ecclesiast
In its step down and wide walk,
Whose cloak is our salve and damp cloth,
                             whose sigh is our medicine . . .

_____

Chipmunk towering like a dinosaur
                          out of the short grass,
Then up the tamarack, sparrow harrowing, then not,
Grasshopper in its thin, green armor,
Short hop, long bound, short hop and a long bound,
Life and death in the milky sunshine now,
                             and concealing shade,
Sparrow avenging machine in the crush of inalterable law.

The arching, drought-dried pilot grasses,
                          earwigged and light-headed,
Nod in the non-wind, directing the small ones nowhere.
Robin lands on the stump root,
Something red and just cut in its beak.
Chipmunk down from the tamarack,
                          and back on patrol,
In and out of the alleyways and sun spots of his saurian world.

The thread that dangles us
                  between a dark and a darker dark,
Is luminous, sure, but smooth sided.
Don't touch it here, and don't touch it there.
                  Don't touch it, in fact, anywhere—
Let it dangle and hold us hard, let it flash and swing.

The urge toward form is the urge toward God,
                    perfection of either
Unhinged, unutterable.
Hot wind in the high country, an east wind, prairie wind.
Unutterable in cathedral or synagogue.
Unhinged, like low wind in high places.
Wind urge and word urge,
                  last form and final thing, the O.

Great mouth. Toothless, untouched.
                  Into whose night sky we all descend.
Star-like we list there
Restructured, forms within forms.
Meanwhile, the morning's sonogram
                  reveals us just as we are,
Birds on their bright courses, the dogs at work in the field,
Flies at the windowpanes, and horses knee-deep in their deep sin.

Hard to forget those autumn evenings
                  driving out to the lake
To catch the sunset,
Harold's wallet already tucked and soft in my coat pocket,
Garda breaking aluminum-like
And curled as the dropping sun sponged out
                  villas and lemon trees,

Gardone shrinking into its own shadow as Friday night came down
Across the water,
Sirmio glittering like an olive leaf
                              turned upside down in the west wind,
Riva gone dark under sunset clouds,
The town of Garda itself
Below us with its fistful of lights beginning to come on,
Pulling us down like a centrifuge to the lake's edge,
Where we parked by the plane tree at the Taverna's door . . .
Those were the days, boys, those were the days.

———————

The bulging blue of July
                              presses us down, and down,
Until the body of the world beneath us slurs to a halt,
Prelapsarian stillness at hand,
Something glistening in the trees,
                              angel wings starting to stir the dust,
The flatness of afternoon
Exacting, a sleep inside a sleep,
Our tongues like turnip greens,
                              our dreams a rodeo dog's.

———————

There is a dearth of spirit as weightless as the grave
That weighs and prefigures us.
It's like the smoke of forest fires from hundreds of miles away
That lies low in the mountains
And will not move,
                              that holds us down with the tiredness of long afternoons,
So weightless the covering, so weightless the spread that spreads it.

There is a desperation for unknown things, a thirst
For endlessness that snakes through our bones

Like a lit fuse looking for Lethe,
                              whose waters reward us,
Their blackness a gossamer and grief
Lifted and laid to one side,
Whose mists are like smoke from forest fires that will not move.

———————

Ravens are flying in and out of the summer woods.
Two, I think, no, three, each buzzed,
                              then buzzed again by a blackbird
Up from the tall reeds by the pond's edge.
The ravens bleat and the blackbirds attack and fall back,
Attack again, the ravens
Upstream by now, little dark points, the blackbirds invisible
As yesterday's prayers.
                    But working hard, Lord, working hard.

Scar Tissue II

Time, for us, is a straight line,
                                   on which we hang our narratives.
For landscape, however, it all is a circling
From season to season, the snake's tail in the snake's mouth,
No line for a story line.
In its vast wheel, in its endless turning,
                                   no lives count, not one.

Hard to imagine that no one counts,
                                   that only things endure.
Unlike the seasons, our shirts don't shed,
Whatever we see does not see us,
                                   however hard we look,
The rain in its silver earrings against the oak trunks,
The rain in its second skin.

Pity the people, Lord, pity their going forth and their coming back,
Pity their sumptuous barricades
                                   against the dark.
Show them the way the dirt works.
Show them its sift, the aftermath and the in-between.
Wet days are their own reward for now,
                                   litter's lapse and the pebble's gleam.

———————

Once in a while, we all succumb
                                   to the merely personal,
Those glass shards and snipped metal
That glitter and disappear and glitter again
                                   in the edged night light

Of memory's anxious sky.
How could it be otherwise, given our histories?

Like Dante's souls of the blessed,
                                        they drop from their tiers
Down to our mind's eye
In whichever heaven it happens to be, for a few words,
An inch of adrenaline,
A slipped heartbeat or so,
                        before they begin to flicker and grain out.

Names, and the names of things, past places,
Lost loves and the love of loss,
The alphabet and geometry of guilt, regret
For things done and things undone,
All of the packaging and misaddresses of our soiled lives—

Ingrid under the archway on Via Giulia,
Quel ramo del Lago di Como,
                        Mt. Ann and the twice-thwarted tower,
Betsy, the White Rabbit, between the columns at Sweet Briar,
San Zeno sun strobe,
                        Goldstein and Thorp,
Flashes like bottle glass, no help for it, flashes like foxfire.

———————

Spirit, subjective correlative and correspondent, moves
Like water under the skin of every story line,
Not too deep, but deep enough,
                                not too close to the top.

There are no words for these words,
Defining and erasing themselves without a sound
Simultaneously,
                larger and smaller, puddle and drift.

In all superstition there lingers a heart of unbelief
For those who walk slip stitch upon the earth
                                        and lose their footprints.
One signs one's name wherever it falls.

———————

The wind never blows in the wrong place,
The sunrise is never late,
                        some Buddhist must certainly have said once.
If not, what a missed sound bite.
The natural world is always in step, and on time,
Absit omen our self-absorption.
Sometimes you eat the bear,
                        and sometimes the bear eats you.

All morning, out of the sunlight, grainy subtraction,
I've courted the shadow life,
Asleep, or half-asleep,
                        like a fish in a deep stream.
Dark spot, bright spot, leopard-skin water.
I feel it drifting around me,
                        my life like a boat
Overhead, floating, unoccupied, back out of sight.

———————

I love to look at the new moon through the bare branches of winter
    trees.
Always the same moon, the same branches,
Always new entrances
                        and caustic geographies.
The stars are still visible, like stunned impurities
In the great sea of anthracite that is the night sky.

One never gets used to this—
Immensity and its absolute,
                        December chill
Like fingernails on the skin—
That something from far away has cracked you,
                                    ever so slightly,
And entered and gone, one never should.

———————

Virginia, Hanover County, December lastlight
Draining into a small hole
Behind the winter wickery
                        of hardwoods and cedar spires
That bordered three fields of soybean stobs
And uncut sumac runners and dead seed millet stalks.

My son and I and the kind man whose acres these were,
Shotgun and bird whirr,
                        day, and the drift of day, sun spill,
I've written it all down in footprints in rubbed red clay,
And put it aside, but find
It's no use, you can't keep anything you can't keep your hands on.

———————

A small rain, a feathery, small rain,
                        has been falling all day
In the neighborhood.
Nothing comes clear, however, nothing is brought to bear.
It snoods our curls, it glosses our lips.
Garbage sacks gleam with a secret light.
                        Low overhead,
Just north of noon, the grey clouds keep on washing their hands
Obsessively, as though they had something still to prove.
1:51 p.m., and all's well

Elsewhere,
            winter settling over the earth like a parachute
From nowhere, pulled open by no one you'd ever know.

Full moon like a 60-watt bulb across the backyard.
This is the light we live in.
This is the light the mind throws
                        against the dark, faint as a finger rub
On a rosary.
It doesn't care how old we are, or where our age will take us.
Nor does the darkness, friend,
                        whose love is a mystery.
Nor does what lies behind it, which isn't.

The outfit was out of town a couple of clicks,
                        on Via Mantovana,
A chain-link fence, a gravelled car park,
Black Chevys, a deuce-and-a-half and a jeep or two
Under the blue Italian sky,
                        all on the q.t.
The 430th CIC Detachment, your tax dollars at work.
Our job was to spy on our own troops and host country.
Great duty for a twenty-three year-old, 1959,
The officers all about to retire after twenty years
Of service, the sergeants too,
Leaving the rest of us to put in our time,
                        two years or four,
Cruising the culture and its sidebars.
On down the road from our light cover,
Just north of Mantova one day after work, Ed DiCenzo and I
Sat in the sunset dripping into the plane trees
                        and Mincio River

Watching an eel fisherman through the trattoria window,
Both eating roast chicken and *tortellini con le gonne*,
The world in its purity and grace,
                              at least for a moment,
Giving our hearts a heads-up and a shoulder to lean on. Great duty.

———————

Sunrise, a cold almost deep enough to crack the oaks,
Morning, like strawberry Kool-Aid,
                              spilling up from the Tidewater.
Middle of January, winter smooth-hipping down the runway.

Hillocks and patches of last week's snow
                              huddle and desiccate across the backyard,
Still white and vaguely funereal in the sweet light.
Squirrel tails flick like beavers', birds sing.

All day the wind will comb out its hair through the teeth of the
      evergreens.
All day the sunlight will sun itself
On the back porch of the cottage, out of the weather.

The world has an infinite beauty, but not, always, for us.
The stars will be boutonnieres,
                              though not necessarily for us.
And the grave is a resting place, but not, however, for one and all.

———————

New skin over old wounds, colorless, numb.
Let the tongue retreat, let the heart be dumb.

3

Appalachia Dog

I can see it still, chopped and channeled, dual pipes,
Metallic red, *Appalachia Dog*
                      in black script on the left front door.
A major ride, dragging the gut in Kingsport in 1952.
A Ford, lowlife and low-down.
Up and back, then left at J. Fred's
                    and west out of town
Into legend and legend's underhalf, its twisted telling.

The rear end was dropped, as though the trunk was leaded for hauling.
Shine running, we said,
Pretending to know something about
                    something we knew nothing about,
Zeke Cleek and the Moose Lodge boys,
                    Junior Johnson's Grey Ghost
Mercury over in North Carolina, the Dog
Flickering in the downtown lights like a candle flame.

We never saw it again.
And over the years, when those days are lifted out
                    from their dark drawers,
The pegged pants with their welt seams, the Mr. B collars,
The Les Paul and Mary Ford 78s broken in half,
That '49 Ford is still there,
                  taillights like nobody's eyes,
Low-riding west toward the rising sun.

Get a Job

Just over sixteen, a cigarette-smoking boy and a bit,
I spent the summer digging ditches,
And carrying heavy things
                    at Bloomingdale School site.
I learned how a backhoe works, and how to handle a shovel,
And multiple words not found in the dictionary.
Sullivan County, Tennessee, a buck twenty an hour,
1952.
        Worst job of my life, but I stuck it out.

Everyone else supported a family, not me.
I was the high school kid, and went home
Each night to my mother's cooking.
                    God knows where the others went.
Mostly across the line into Scott County, Virginia, I think,
Appalachian appendix, dead end.
Slackers and multipliers, now in, now out of jail, on whom I depended.
Cold grace for them.
            God rest them all road ever they offended,

To rhyme a prominent priest.
                    Without a ministry, without portfolio,
Each morning I sought them out
For their first instructions, for their laying on of hands.
I wish I could say that summer changed my life,
                            or changed theirs,
But it didn't. Apparently, nothing ever does.
I did, however, leave a skin there.
A bright one, I'm told, but less bright than its new brother.

Archaeology

The older we get, the deeper we dig into our childhoods,
Hoping to find the radiant cell
That washed us, and caused our lives
                              to glow in the dark like clock hands
Endlessly turning toward the future,
Tomorrow, day after tomorrow, the day after that,
                              all golden, all in good time.

Hiwassee Dam, North Carolina.
                              Still 1942,
Still campfire smoke in both our eyes, my brother and I
Gaze far out at the lake in sunflame,
Expecting our father at any moment, like Charon, to appear
Back out of the light from the other side,
          low-gunwaled and loaded down with our slippery dreams.

Other incidents flicker like foxfire in the black
Isolate distance of memory,
                              cross-eyed, horizon-haired.
Which one, is it one, is it any one that cleans us, clears us,
That relimbs our lives to a shining?

One month without rain, two months,
                              third month of the new year,
Afternoon breeze-rustle dry in the dry needles of hemlock and pine.
I can't get down deep enough.
Sunlight flaps its enormous wings and lifts off from the backyard,
The wind rattles its raw throat,
                              but I still can't go deep enough.

The Sodbuster's Saloon and Hall of Fame

Each time they knock one back,
                              another longhorn kneels in the dust.
Each time they settle up, another strand of barbed wire
Is stretched to the vanishing point,
                              that staked and stalled horizon.

Outside, their horse-and-wagons,
                              in slow motion toward paradise,
Turn west at the edge of town.
They take a loose rein, they take a deep seat
                              and give the horses their heads,

Dipped in their rodeo dreams:
                              Up next
Out of chute no. 1 on Upside Down, Amos Many Wounds,
His belt buckle big as the moon,
                              and sharp-edged, and glistening like wire points in the sun.

Heraclitean Backwash

Wherever I am,
        I always wonder what I am doing back there,
Strange flesh in a stranger land.
As though the world were a window and I a faint reflection
Returning my gaze
Wherever I looked, and whatever I looked upon.

Absence of sunlight, white water among the tall trees.
Nothing whispers its secret.
Silence, for some, is a kind of healing, it's said,
        for others the end of a dark road
That begins the zone of a greater light.
Fish talk to the dead in the shallow water below the hill.

Or so the Egyptian thought,
        who knew a thing or two about such things.
Strange flesh in a stranger land.
The clouds take their toll.
Like moist souls, they litter the sky on their way to where they're not.
Dandelions scatter across the earth,
        fire points, small sunsqualls.

(For H.V., fixed point in the flux)

High Country Spring

It's not so much the description, it's what you describe,
Green pox on the aspen limbs,
Lilac bud-bursts set to go off,
                              suppuration of late May.

The world is a tiny object, a drop of pine sap,
Amber of robin's beak, like that,
                              backlit by sunlight,
Pulling the glow deep inside.

China Traces

Nature contains no negatives.
                              Nothing is lost there,
The word is. Except the word.

In spring there is autumn in my heart,
My spirit, outside of nature, like slow mist in the trees,
Looking for somewhere to dissipate.

I write out my charms and spells
Against the passage of light
                              and gathering evil
Each morning. Each evening hands them back.

Out of the nothing nothing comes.
                              The rain keeps falling,
As we expected, the bitter and boundaryless rain.
The grass leaves no footprints,
                              the creek keeps on eating its one word.

In the night, the light assembles the stars
                              and tightens their sash.

Matins

Sunlight like Vaseline in the trees,
       smear and shine, smear and shine.
Ten days of rain and now the echoing forth of blank and blue
Through the evergreens.
Deer stand on their hind legs
      in the bright meadow grasses.
The sound of the lilac upsurge rings bells for the bees.
Cloud puffs, like mortar rounds from the afterlife,
         pockmark the sky.
Time, in its crystal goblet, laps and recedes, laps and recedes.

If we were the Rapture's child, if we
Were the Manichaean boy,
If we were the Bodhisattva baby,
      today would be a good day
To let the light in, or send it out.
We're not, however. We're Nature's nobodies,
       and we'd do well
To put on the *wu wei* slippers and find a hard spot
To sit on,
   sinking like nothing through the timed tides of ourselves.

North

This is the north, cloud tatters trailing their joints across the ground
And snagging themselves
In the soaked boughs of the evergreens.
Even the heart could lift itself higher than they do,
The soaked and bough-spattered heart,
But doesn't because this is the north,
Where everything dark, desire and its extra inch, holds back
And drags itself, sullen and misty-mouthed, through the trees.
An apparitionless afternoon,
One part water, two parts whatever the light won't give us up.

The north is not the memory of the north but its repeat
And cadences, St. Augustine in blackface, and hand to mouth:
The north is where we go when there's no place left to go.
It's where our altered selves are,
Resplendent and unrepentant and wholly unrecognizable.
We've been here for years,
Fog-rags and rain and sun spurts,
Beforeworlds behind us, slow light spots like Jimmy Durante's fade-out
Hopscotching across the meadow grass.
This is our landscape and our landing zone, this is our dark glass.

In Praise of Franz Kafka

Weather no matter, time no matter,
The immemorially long and windy body of the Hunter Gracchus
Floats again
Through the buoyant dark of the pine forest,
                                    ship-borne and laid out
Like a downed larch on the black, intransitive deckwork.
He passes each year
On the waters that circle above the earth
In his pitiless turn and endless geography.
The wings of the crewmen hang like washing along the railing.
June is his sunlight, and June is his farthering forth,
His world pure circumference.
                        Follow him if you can.

Vespers

Who wouldn't wish to become
The fiery life of divine substance
                        blazing above the fields,
Shining above the waters,
The rain like dust through his fingerbones,
All our yearning like flames in his feathery footprints?
Who, indeed?
            And still . . .

The world in its rags and ghostly raiment calls to us
With grinding and green gristle
Wherever we turn,
                and we are its grist, and we are its groan.
Over the burned lightning strikes of tree shadows
                        branded across the near meadow,
Over the dusk-dazed heads of the oat grass,
The bullbat's chortle positions us, and holds us firm.

We are the children of the underlife,
                    at least for a time,
Flannel shirt on a peg, curled
Postcards from years past
                thumbtacked along the window frames.
Outside, deer pause on the just-cut grass,
The generator echoes our spirit's humdrum,
                        and gnats drone high soprano . . .
Not much of a life, but I'll take it.

The Narrow Road to the Distant City

Heap me, Lord, heap me, we're heard to say,
Not really meaning it, but meaning
Gently, my man, ever so gently,
                              please lay me down,
Allow me all things I've not deserved,
Dandle my heart and tell me I'm still your baby boy.

How could it be otherwise,
                    our just meat being ash,
Which, don't worry, is set to be served at the next course.
We've said grace in the past tense.
We've said our prayers out of our mouths,
                              not out of our hearts.
The more we talked, the more our tongues tied.

So pay us some nevermind.
Let us pretend the world's our own dream,
And be unto us as a hard wind
                    that understands nothing.
In fact, be yourself,
If that is what the nothing that is,
                    and the nothing that is to come, is called for.

Pilgrim's Progress

At the start, it goes like this—
One's childhood has a tremendous shape,
                              and moves like a wild animal
Through the deadfall and understory.
It's endlessly beautiful,
                    elusive and on to something.
It hides out, but never disappears.

Later, the sacred places Delphi and Italy on us,
Flicking and flashing through the forest,
                              half-seen, half-remembered.
And with them the woods itself,
Each tree, each interlude of marsh grass and beaver shade
Something to tug the sleeve with.

In the end, of course, one's a small dog
At night on the front porch,
                    barking into the darkness
At what he can't see, but smells, somehow, and is suspicious of.
Barking, poor thing, and barking,
With no one at home to call him in,
                         with no one to turn the light on.

Little Landscape

To lighten the language up, or to dark it back down
Becomes the blade edge we totter on.
To say what is true and clean,
                                    to say what is secret and underground,
To say the things joy can't requite, and to say them well . . .

This is the first conundrum.
The second is like unto it,
                                    the world is a link and a like:
One falls and all falls.
In this last light from midsummer's week,
                                    who knows which way to go?

The great blue heron wheels up the meadow
                                    and folds into Basin Creek.
Only the fish know which angle his shadow will make.
And what they know is not what he knows,
Which is neither light nor dark nor joy,
                                    but is just is, just is.

Ghost Days

Labyrinthine, Byzantine,
                    memory's gold-ground mosaics
Still spill us and drop us short.
Who was the sixth guy in the Fiat 500
With Giancarlo, Pamela, the two drunken Carabinieri and me
That New Year's Eve around 3 a.m.
Circling the Colosseum
                    and circling the Colosseum?
And what year was it ten inches of snow descended
Like papal grace on Rome, and all the small *macchine*
Crashed on the Tiber's retaining wall?
                              What year was that?
The pieces clear and occlude like a retinal bleed.

And where are you now, Giancarlo,
                    my first Italian friend,
Mad *marinaio* of the Via Margutta, where are you?
Like a black blot in a troubled eye,
                    you fall into place, then fall out
From the eyeball's golden dome.
How high you hung there once in our fast-faltering younger days.
How high we all hung,
                    artificial objects in artificial skies,
Our little world like a little S. Apollinare in Classe,
Weedy and grass-gripped outside,
                    white and glare-gold within,
Our saints with their wings missing,
But shining, nevertheless,
                    as darkness gathers the darkness, and holds it tight.

The Silent Generation III

These are our voices, active, passive and suppressed,
                                and these are our syllables.
We used them to love your daughters, we used them to love your sons.
We travelled, we stayed home, we counted our days out
                                like prescription pills.
In the end, like everyone, we had too much to say.

———————

We lived by the seat of our pants, we bet on the come
Only to come up short,
                and see, as the smoke began to clear,
The life we once thought that boundless canopy of sky,
Was just the sound of an axe, echoing in the woods.

———————

We hadn't the heart for heartlessness,
                                we hadn't the salt or the wound.
The words welled,
                but goodness and mercy declined to follow us.
We carried our wings on our own backs, we ate our dead.
Like loose lightbulbs, we kept our radiance to ourselves.

———————

Not heavy enough to be the hangman's burden,
                                our noosed names
Are scrawled in the dust discursively, line after line.
Too strange for our contemporaries,
                we'll prove to be
Not strange enough for posterity.

O you who come after us,
Read our remains,

            study the soundless bones and do otherwise.

Time Will Tell

Time was when time was not,
                        and the world an uncut lawn
Ready for sizing. We looked, and took the job in hand.
Birds burst from our fingers, cities appeared, and small towns
In the interim.
                        We loved them all.
In distant countries, tides nibbled our two feet on pebbly shores
With their soft teeth and languorous tongues.
Words formed and flew from our fingers.
                                    We listened and loved them all.

Now finitude looms like antimatter, not this and not that,
And everywhere, like a presence one bumps into,
Oblivious, unwittingly,
                        Excuse me, I beg your pardon.
But time has no pardon to beg, and no excuses.

The wind in the meadow grasses,
                            the wind through the rocks,
Bends and breaks whatever it touches.
It's never the same wind in the same spot, but it's still the wind,
And blows in its one direction,
                            northwest to southeast,
An ointment upon the skin, a little saliva,
Time with its murderous gums and pale, windowless throat,
Its mouth pressed to our mouths,
                        pushing the breath in, pulling it out.

Hawksbane

There are things that cannot be written about, journeys
That cannot be taken they are so sacred and long.

There is no nature in eternity, no wind shift, no weeds.

Whatever our vision, whatever our implement,
We looked in the wrong places, we looked for the wrong things.

We are not what is new, we are not what we have found.

The Woodpecker Pecks, but the Hole Does Not Appear

It's hard to imagine how unremembered we all become,
How quickly all that we've done
Is unremembered and unforgiven,
                         how quickly
Bog lilies and yellow clover flashlight our footfalls,
How quickly and finally the landscape subsumes us,
And everything that we are becomes what we are not.

This is not new, the orange finch
And the yellow and dun finch
                        picking the dry clay politely,
The grasses asleep in their green slips
Before the noon can roust them,
The sweet oblivion of the everyday
                          like a warm waistcoat
Over the cold and endless body of memory.

Cloud-scarce Montana morning.
July, with its blue cheeks puffed out like a *putto* on an ancient map,
Huffing the wind down from the northwest corner of things,
Tweets on the evergreen stumps,
                       swallows treading the air,
The ravens hawking from tree to tree, *not you, not you,*
Is all that the world allows, and all one could wish for.

Singing Lesson

This is the executioner's hour,
                                        deep noon, hard light,
Everything edge and horizon-honed,
Windless and hushed, as though a weight were about to fall,
And shadows begin to slide from beneath things, released
In their cheap suits and eager to spread.

Out in the meadow, nothing breathes,
                                        the deer seem to stop
Mid-jump at the fence, the swallows hanging like little hawks in the air.
The landscape loosens a bit, and softens.
                                        Like miniature exhalations,
Wind stirs in the weeds, a dog barks, the shadows stretch and seep out.

Therefore, when the Great Mouth with its two tongues of water and ash
Shall say, Suffer the darkness,
Suffer the darkness to come unto you,
                                        suffer its singsong,
And you will abide,
Listen to what the words spell, listen and sing the song.

NOTES

"Images from the Kingdom of Things": Witter Bynner, *The Jade Mountain* in *The Chinese Translations*, Farrar, Straus and Giroux, 1978.

"Against the American Grain": As Hopkins might have called it, an 'inscape of being.'

"Saturday Morning Satori": Wei Ying-wu, in *The Chinese Translations*.

"Wrong Notes": Ibid.

"Heraclitean Backwash": Heraclitus, *Fragments*, translated by Brooks Haxton, Penguin Books, 2001.

"Matins": '*Wu wei*': In Taoism and Zen Buddhism, unmotivated action; in Chinese, literally, 'nondoing.' (Robert Denham in *Northrop Frye Unbuttoned*, Gnomon Press, Frankfort, KY, 2004.)

"Vespers": Hildegard of Bingen, *Selected Writings*, translated by Mark Atherton, Penguin Books, 2001.

"Hawksbane": Matsuo Bashō, *The Narrow Road to the Deep North and Other Travel Sketches*, translated by Nobuyuki Yuasa, Penguin Books, 1966.

Printed in the USA
CPSIA information can be obtained
at www.ICGtesting.com
LVHW091148150724
785511LV00005B/614